marques vickers

UNSEEN WATERWAYS OF MARIN COUNTY

UNSEEN MARIN COUNTY WATERWAYS

Marques Vickers

**MARQUIS PUBLISHING
HERRON ISLAND, WASHINGTON**

Version 1

Published by Marquis Publishing
Herron Island, WA

Vickers, Marques, 1957

UNSEEN MARIN COUNTY WATERWAYS

Dedicated To My Daughters Charline and Caroline

UNSEEN MARIN: The Waterways of Marin County, California

Preface

MILL VALLEY:
Pickleweed Inlet
Coyote Creek
Corte Madera del Presidio
Mill Creek

CENTRAL MARIN COUNTY:
Corte Madera Creek
Tamalpais Creek
Larkspur Creek
Ross Creek
San Anselmo Creek

SAN RAFAEL AND FAIFAX:
Fairfax Creek
Las Gallinas Creek
San Rafael Creek
Sleepy Hollow Creek
Santa Venetia Marsh

Preface

This edition is a photographic journey tracing each of Marin County's fourteen principle waterways from their source to termination point. The sequence of images follows this course making it a stride-by-stride accompaniment with the camera lens.

The creeks and streams that eminently flow throughout Marin County are important draining outlets originating from the elevated mountain ranges that frame the skeleton of the region. Each creek becomes an important tributary that ultimately flows into the San Francisco Bay. Marin County has one of the highest rainfall averages in the San Francisco Bay area and flooding has been a constant throughout its history.

The Coastal Miwok tribe inhabited the territory of Marin County for hundreds of years harvesting and gathering crops, hunting and fishing for salmon and steelhead trout. Their population was speculated to be near 5,000 and their lands stretched from Marin to southern Sonoma county and Bodega Bay.

With the encroachment by Spanish settlers and missionaries and the creation of Missions San Francisco de Asis and San Rafael, the native population became depleted to 300 by 1848 and 60 by 1880. The principle cause for their demise became their exposure to European diseases, which their immune systems could not resist. The remains of a settlement and the burial site of their leader Chief Marin were unearthed near the juncture of Sycamore and Locust Streets in Mill Valley.

With the ascension of the Mexican government, which wrested their independence from Spain, the missions were closed. The new government divided the region into two separate land grants in the 1830s.

Over the subsequent two centuries, the region would evolve into upscale suburban enclaves with Mount Tamalpais looming prominently in the background. One might easily imagine an earlier rustic landscape clotted with dense forests. Corte de Madera is translated from the Spanish into a *place where wood is cut* and Mill Valley was renowned for its celebrated sawmill. The structure still remains along Mill Creek.

Within the tenure of this photography project, I had the opportunity to witness the duality of each waterway's existence. For most of the year, the creeks remain docile and placidly flowing. When I began photographing, California was in the midst of a devastating five-year drought. Water levels had recessed to dangerously low stages.

During March 2016, forecasted El Nino rains drenched Marin County for a ten-day period with steady and substantial rains. This followed a February with no rainfall. The sluggish creeks suddenly swelled and an abrupt surge radically transformed their appearance. The calm streams resembled raging rivers. The crystalline waters became muddied by sediment. Nature had reawakened from five years of dormancy and draught.

During this stretch, excess floodwaters fortunately did not materialize. One day they ultimately will as they have for generations and centuries. These untamable bodies of water cannot be fully constricted within the confines of city planning and construction development. Portions flow under commercial and residential structures and offer residents an alluring picturesque view. The pleasure is tempered by an uneasy truce once torrential rains resume.

Each creek seems uniquely distinct and many sustain foliage and fauna that augment the splendor. Most are easily accessible and feature adjacent hiking trails. Sections remain concealed by private property constructions.

The Marin waterways are a poignant reminder that no matter how resolute mankind attempts to subdue nature, the temporarily vanquished will ultimately prevail.

Pickleweed Inlet

Pickleweed Inlet is a small bay that begins at Roque Moraes Drive and widens southward through a parkland basin area that includes Hauke and Bayfront Parks. The waters of the Corte Madera del Presidio empty from the west and Coyote Creek from the southwest before the Inlet flows into Richardson Bay. Richardson Bay ultimately merges into the San Francisco Bay.

Coyote Creek

Coyote Creek begins on Coyote Ridge at the south end of the Bothin Marsh and traces Tennessee Valley Road. At the intersection of Tennessee Valley and Marin Avenue, a western tributary stream empties into the main creek. The tributary divide follows the course of Marin Avenue before the juncture. At the termination of Tennessee Valley Road, the 2.1-mile creek runs parallel with the Shoreline Highway before ultimately flowing into the Pickleweed Inlet that empties into Richardson and the San Francisco Bays.

Corte Madera del Presidio

Corte Madera del Presidio originates as a draining outlet on the eastern slope of Mount Tamalpais running southbound along West Blithedale Avenue. The 4.1-mile-long creek then splits between West Blithedale to the north and Corte Madera Avenue to the south until it passes underneath downtown Mill Valley until Miller Avenue. At Valley Circle, the waters of the Mill Creek converge with the Corte Madera del Presidio.

The flow continues bordered by Sycamore Avenue to the north and Miller Avenue to the south. Plymouth Avenue briefly lines its northern bank. The creek passes under Camino Alto before dividing into a watershed park area. The waters empty into the Pickleweed Inlet, which ultimately flows out to Richardson Bay.

Mill Creek

Mill Creek originates as a draining outlet on the eastern slope of Mount Tamalpais, converging with Cascade Creek at Cascade Falls. The creek follows Cascade Drive in the southeasterly direction culminating at Old Mill Park and an original Sawmill dating back to the 1830s. The creek runs east along Throckmorton Avenue and empties into `the Arroyo Corte Madera del Presidio between Miller Avenue to the south and Laurelwood Avenue to the north.

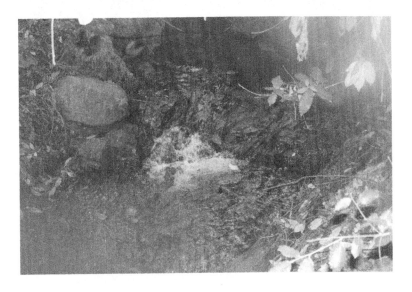

115

Corte Madera Creek

Corte Madera Creek extends approximately 4.5 miles beginning at a conjuncture with Ross Creek between Sir Francis Drake Boulevard and the cul-de-sac of Locust Avenue in Ross.

The creek traces the routing of Sir Francis Drake Boulevard southward skirting behind the College of Marin and crossing under College Avenue in Kentfield. After Stadium Avenue, it widens southward into the Ross Valley until it emerges adjacent to Creekside Park to the north and Harvard Drive to the south. In Kentfield at an elbow bend of the creek, the Tamalpais Creek empties into the stream from the west.

The creek passes under the Bon Air Road Bridge before tracing portions of Magnolia Avenue to the south in Larkspur and South Eliseo Drive in Corte Madera to the north. Between Redwood High School and the Bon Air Shopping Center in Greenbrae and adjacent to Piper Park, the Larkspur Creek empties into the Corte Madera Creek.

The Corte Madera Creek widens and is surrounded by waterfront properties on both banks before passing under a Highway 101 Overpass Bridge. The creek empties into Richardson Bay and then the San Francisco Bay near San Quentin State Prison.

151

Tamalpais Creek

Along an elevated hillside of Woodland Place in Kentfield, the Tamalpais Creek winds eastward along Woodland Road. Just beyond the conclusion of Woodside Road near College Avenue (which becomes Magnolia Avenue) the diminutive creek empties into the Corte Madera Creek.

Larkspur Creek

Larkspur Creek flows 3.5 miles originating in the Baltimore Canyon Open Space Preserve. The creek winds southward along Dawn Falls Trail before tracing the Redwood tree lined Madrone Avenue and crossing under and following Magnolia Avenue briefly in Larkspur.

The creek then follows Rose Lane before narrowing at Doherty Drive and merging into the Corte Madera Creek. The town of Larkspur was mistakenly named by Georgiana Wright, the wife of an area developer in the 1880's after the abundant lupine flowers. Wright misidentified them as larkspur flowers.

Ross Creek

The Miwok tribes left seven ceremonial mounds in the present town of Ross. The town derived its name from a Tasmanian immigrant, James Ross, who made his fortune selling liquor to gold panners and prospectors in San Francisco.

Ross Creek originates just south before Phoenix Lake, whose overflow spills into the creek. The creek follows Lagunitas Road in Ross until a deviation that aligns its with The Branson School and Hillgirt Drive. Its path crosses Norwood Avenue and Shady Lane before spilling into a concrete aqueduct and convergence of the Corte Madera and San Anselmo Creeks just east of Locust Avenue.

San Anselmo Creek

The small and isolated Cascade Creek located in the eastern flank of the Pine Mountain Ridge culminates at Cascade Falls. This extremity begins the southern descent of the San Anselmo Creek. The creek forms the southern sector of the Cascade Canyon Open Space Preserve and follows Cascade Drive to the east. At the juncture of Cascade Drive and Bolinas Road, the creek follows Dominga Avenue before tracing Lansdale Avenue and passing south of Sir Francis Drake High School.

At the southeastern corner of Drake High, the Sleepy Hollow Creek feeds into the San Anselmo Creek. The creek follows Sir Francis Drake Boulevard through downtown San Anselmo until finally converging with the Ross and Corte Madera Creeks between Sir Francis Drake Boulevard and the cul-de-sac of Locust Avenue in the town of Ross. Downtown San Anselmo has an extended history of flooding when the creek overflows its constricted banks.

Fairfax Creek

Fairfax Creek is one of the few Marin water bodies that does not empty into one of the larger streams at its termination. The creek commences between Baywood Canyon Road and Deer Creek Court in Fairfax near the Loma Alta Open Space Preserve. It then flows eastward along Sir Francis Drake Boulevard.

At the intersection of Olema Road and Sir Francis Drake Boulevard, it straddles both roadways weaving into downtown Fairfax. It terminates at Winnie Bank Street adjacent to the Contratti Park Baseball Field and Fairfax Town Office.

Las Gallinas Creek

The Las Gallinas Creek begins in the hills of Terra Linda just west of Circle Road between Indian Road and Oak View Drive in San Rafael. The creek follows Circle Road before passing under Los Ranchitos Road and following El Prado Avenue. It continues northward along Merrydale Road before passing under an overpass on Highway 101.

The South Fork then follows McInnis Parkway in the Gallinas Watershed terrain before spilling into the Santa Venetia Marsh Preserve. The waters then empty into the western sector of the San Pablo Bay.

247

San Rafael Creek

San Rafael Creek originates at the intersection of Bayview Street and Albert Park Lane in San Rafael. It continues eastward on Albert Park Lane until mounting north on Lindaro Street briefly and crossing under Anderson Drive, Lincoln Avenue and Francisco Boulevard West.

The creek's flow continues parallel to Second Street, which ultimately merges into Third Street. The creek then becomes a causeway lined on both sides by commercial constructions and the Municipal Yacht Harbor.

At the juncture of Third Street and Point San Pedro Road, the creek bends and follows a watercourse with Point San Pedro Road to the north and Canal Street to the south. Residential structures replace commercial and the creek passes the Marin Yacht Club to the north. Widening, the waters flow into San Rafael Bay, which empties into the San Francisco Bay.

Sleepy Hollow Creek

Sleepy Hollow Creek begins adjacent to Butterfield Road in San Anselmo and traces the roadway in the southeasterly direction before spilling into San Anselmo Creek just south of Sir Francis Drake High School.

The Santa Venetia Marsh Preserve

The Santa Venetia Marsh Preserve is a 33-acre salt marsh surrounded by a levee. The region is part of the Las Gallinas creek delta watershed that drains the Terra Linda valleys. The marsh was diked and filled in the early 1900s when the adjacent area was leveled for development.

The surrounding area is now a patchwork of channels, marshland and flood control areas inhabited by a diverse array of birds and animals. Gallinas Creek forms the northern border of the Preserve and a series of San Rafael cul-de-sacs that end along its southern banks. These roads include Vendola Drive, Rincon Way, Hacienda Way, Descanso Way, Estancia Way, Palmera Way and La Play Way. Vendola Drive winds around to form its eastern border.

291

Author, photographer and visual artist Marques Vickers was born in 1957 in Vallejo, California. He graduated from Azusa Pacific University in Los Angeles and became the Public Relations and Executive Director for the Burbank, California Chamber of Commerce between 1979-84.

Professionally, he has operated travel, apparel, wine, rare book and publishing businesses. His paintings and sculptures have been exhibited in art galleries, private collections and museums in the United States and Europe. He has previously lived in the Burgundy and Languedoc regions of France and currently lives in the South Puget Sound region of Western Washington.

He has written and published over one hundred books spanning a diverse variety of subjects including true crime, international travel, social satire, wine production, architecture, history, fiction, auctions, fine art, poetry and photojournalism.

He has two daughters, Charline and Caroline who reside in Europe.

Made in the USA
Las Vegas, NV
27 December 2023

83607803R00173